OUR FIGHT
Juliana Muniz Westcott

ISBN: 9781793258366
Imprint: Independently published

The profits from this sale will go towards
supporting Extinction Rebellion

For Ester and Sara

OUR FIGHT

Juliana Muniz Westcott

My parents and teachers tell us to be kind, to be polite.
I trust them in those things as normally they are right.

Then we learned how oceans are crowded with the plastic we throw away, and how we still make all these things that end up in the bay.

Then we heard about climate change and about the animals we lost, about the ones who are almost gone and how the world is on defrost.

Now we're learning something new: sometimes we need to fight.

Fight for the animals, the insects, the trees,
fight for truth and what's right.

extinction rebellion

But this fight is a peaceful one, a fight for you and me. We need to raise the alarm so everyone can see.

The world is getting warmer every year and we urgenty need to protect our biosphere.

So our fight is for the
Black Rhino
whose horn is not ours.

Our voice rises for the
Giant Panda
so their habitat
does not disappear.

Vunerable

Our hearts reach out to the
Amur Leopard
We will let them know,
they're not forgotten
in all that snow.

Critically
Endangered

Hear us **Giant Ibis**
you are not alone,
Your wetlands will be restored,
that will be our milestone.

Critically
Endangered

Stay with us
African Penguin
we will give you some good rest,
we will close down those beaches
and make sure tourists don't
step on your nests.

Gorgeous **Grevy's Zebra**
do not be in distress,
our fight against hunting
will come to a success.

Dear **Puffin**
do not be afraid,
We'll make sure you will
have fish back on your plate.

Endangered

Wise **Asian Elephant**
do not leave us now.
We'll give you back your land,
you can trust us it's a vow.

Endangered

Near Threatened

Playful **Narwals**
I know it is getting hot
but stay close to the ice
we will hold back this defrost.

Slow down dear **Pygmy Three-toed Sloth**, keep resting in this tree, we will make sure, yes we will, your home will stay right here.

Critically Endangered

Cute little **Hedgehog**
please keep on the move,
we will make holes in our fences,
and keep your hedgerows safe,
we know you will approve.

Least
Concern

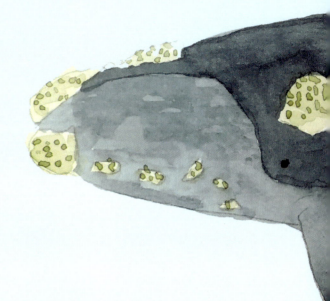

My dear friend North
Atlantic Right Whale,
we are here for you now,
do not cry we will not fail.

extinction
rebellion

So we will sit down on bridges, block traffic and gather in
squares.

We will make sure they hear us,
yes they will hear us everywhere.

The time for denial is over, it is time to act. This is our Earth, this is our fight.

The world is on the brink of climate breakdown and a sixth mass extinction. We face catastrophe if we do not act fast enough.

Join the Extinction Rebellion today.

extinction
rebellion

Printed in Poland
by Amazon Fulfillment
Poland Sp. z o.o., Wrocław